Railways in your Garden

A hobby for all ages. Jordan Bryan, aged 1 year 9 months, with granddad's pride and joy.

RAILWAYS IN YOUR GARDEN

edited by
David Pratt & David Joy

ATLANTIC PUBLISHERS
Trevithick House, West End, Penryn, Cornwall, TR10 8HE

First published 1994
in association with Garden Railway Specialists, Princes Risborough

Reprinted 1998

Contributors: Michael Adamson, David Gray, David Joy,
David & Becky Pinniger, David Pratt, Derek Shephard

This edition 2001
Text revised by David Pratt, with illustrations selected by David Joy

ISBN: 1 902827 01 5

Design and layout: Trevor Ridley
Printed by The Amadeus Press, Bradford, West Yorkshire

Cover photographs:
Front: 16mm scale Campbeltown & Machrihanish Railway 0-6-2T *Atlantic*, built by John Shawe.
(David Pinniger)
Back: G Scale Zillertal 0-6-2T by LGB, happily coping with a rare snowfall on a line near Blackpool.
(Allan Judd)

Picture credits (T = top; L = lower):- Bachmann Industries 10T; David Baker 39, 69; Tim Bowis 33; Huub Brech 26; Terence Bryan 2; Keith Chadwick 25; Jack Clarke 14; John Clover 75L; Geoffrey Dix 49; David Edgley 76; Malcolm Edwards 74; Ken Elliott 60; Philip Elwin 79; Don Fenton 10L; Don Froud 84L; Gauge 3 Society 7, 12L; Tag Gorton 16L, 81L, 85; David Gray 51; Pete Hilsden 93; David Jenkinson 24L; David Joy 9T, 17, 21L, 24T, 28B, 41, 44L, 48L, 53, 70, 73; Barry C. Lane 63; Philip Lane 44T, 52T; Lawson Little 28T; Laurie Maunder 31; Martyn Mitchell 68; Tony Morris 96; Rex Mountfield 37; Geoff Munday 56; Fraser Neilson 48T; Piko 77; David Pinniger 9L, 21T, 52L, 67, 78, 84T; Derek Pollard 64T, 65; Graham Powell 12T; John Powers, Hobbybahn 20; David Pratt 11,13, 27, 29, 38, 43, 64L, 79, 89; Jack Ray 18; Peter Harvatt Robinson 30; Stephen Robinson 72; Trevor Shephard 75T; Michael Taylor 16T; Peter Trinder 62; Stephen J. Tucker 81T; John Wenlock 35, 88L; John Whisson 45, 88T, 90; Graham Wilkins, 87; Michael Woodward 55, 80, 91

Drawing on page 8 by permission of Brandbright Ltd.

Contents

Introduction

There are many reasons that we find ourselves modelling railways. For those of us who are the older generation, the remembrance of steam as the main motive power is very strong. For us the sight of dozens of large and small locomotives at a main line terminus, the overhanging pall of smoke, the sounds, the smell of coal and hot oil, are all etched into our memories.

The younger, and the very young among us, will have visited preserved railways, travelled on narrow gauge lines, or up snow-covered mountains on ski-ing holidays. Perhaps you will have been introduced to the hobby with a small scale railway of your own, perhaps 'Double-O' in the loft, or 'O-gauge' handed down by elders.

Engineers among us will relish the challenge of creating in miniature a locomotive that weighed in at over a hundred tons, pulled a thousand tons or travelled at 126 miles an hour by boiling water. The principles are very simple, the engineering very sophisticated and the design captured us all. We call it 'live steam' and discuss endlessly the attributes that make a steam locomotive 'alive'. You only have to stand near one, as small children love to do – to feel the warmth, to know that it is alive, feeding on coal and drinking water.

We might prefer to run some of the super expresses of the modern world, from Japan or Europe, electric or diesel. Even a replica of a real railway that we know – from Alaska or India, or create our own personalised railway company and operations.

But why in the garden? The boom in garden interest and products, television programmes and publications is apparent to all of us. The garden is now an extension of our homes, a place for the family to relax and play. We design and build our gardens with advice from professional personalities. For many of us it is possibly the largest space at our disposal at home. When we have acquired the plants, patio, the pond, the lights – we look for movement and interest as we sit and relax in our own creation, away from the stress of

the real world.

A garden railway provides interest for all the family. The children can plant, supervised by the lady of the house. Rockeries are always popular and provide detail in a larger scheme of planting and railway planning. The heavy work of surveying, levelling and permanent way construction leads to the acquisition of new skills – how do you level the track at far sides of the garden? Or grade the rails up an incline of 1:100, 1:10 for the mountain rack railway? Or bridge that pond?

The permanent way, and tunnels, buildings all need to withstand our climate and the seasons. Although small, this will be a real railway. There will be rain, frost, leaves. The railway will be attacked by wildlife – and some younger humans. Some of the skills gained in construction will apply equally well to real buildings.

This hobby, spanning electronics to soil mechanics, via horticulture and civil engineering, must have it all. Whatever the ages and interests of the

Garden railways traditional style. The stout timber supports, Gauge 3 track and the locomotive, made by Carson prior to 1920, recall the early days of the hobby. Despite the vintage appearance, the photograph was taken in 1997. Gauge 3 is now enjoying a revival.

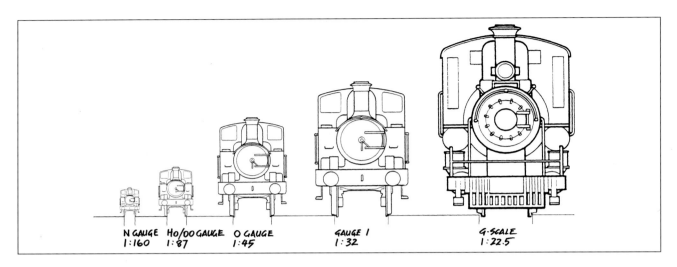

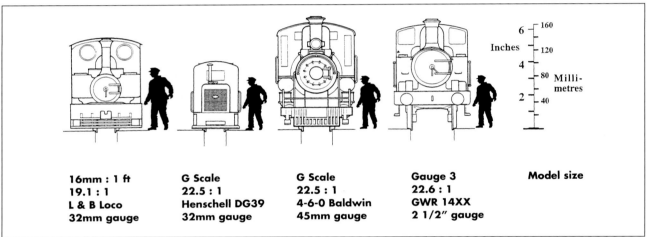

Opposite: The two most popular scales for scenic garden railways.
Top: G Scale, with narrow gauge prototypes modelled at around 1:22.5 and running on Gauge 1 (45mm) track. An LGB Wismar railbus is maintaining winter services.
Lower: 16mm Scale also models narrow gauge lines but at 1:19 on Gauge 0 (32mm) track. The narrower track width suits 2ft gauge prototypes, as here with this Lynton & Barnstaple 2-6-2T Lew. It is seen on the Border Counties Railway, the pioneer creation of Jack Wheldon.

partcicipants. This is an interest and hobby for most of us that may be easily begun but usually stays with us for life.

Scales

Garden railways have been built in many scales over the last seventy years of the hobby's existence. There have been attempts at 'Double-O' as the smallest that might be successful right through 'Three-inch' to 'Five-inch', both as 'ride-on' and pure modeling in a very large scale. Common scales in use include Gauge 0 (1:43), popularised by Hornby and Bassett-Lowke in both clockwork and electric forms; and Gauge 1 (1:32) which has even older roots in Carette and Bing, with Marklin still going strong and even producing tinplate.

In 1967 E.P.Lehman Patentwerk of Nuremburg introduced the Lehman Grossbahn (LGB) with a track and gauge the same as Gauge 1 (45mm), but not standard gauge models. The narrow gauge prototypes are modelled at around 1:22.5 scale. This has assumed the title of G Scale and several

manufacturers have produced to this scale and slight variations from it. Most G Scale prototypes are metre, three foot or three foot six inch gauge, and occasionally two foot six railways are modelled. 16mm to the foot scale railways are usually modelled from two-foot gauge prototypes.

At the turn of the Millenium there are more widely available models in Gauge Three (also known as G64). These are standard gauge models that run on 2½ (64mm) spaced rails and can be combined with the narrow gauge G Scale models on their 45mm spaced rails. Accessories and buildings for both scales are the same.

There are similarities between G Scale and 16mm, both of which model narrow gauge prototypes. However, the latter runs on 32mm spaced rails with a scale of 1:19.

G Scale has come to dominate the garden railway scene. This is because of wide availability, popularity of the railways modelled – European and American – and the quality of the weather resistant plastic products. Gauge 1 (on the same track) has seen some of the finest live steam model locomotive engineering in metal, and for this reason is also a popular choice with a wide ranging supply of accessories.

The price of entrance to the hobby can be quite small, comparable to indoor 'Double-O'. This is perhaps where we all might have started.

Opposite, top: The scale of 1:20.3 (15mm to the foot) is rapidly growing in popularity among USA modellers as it accurately represents 3ft gauge prototypes. It has been adopted by Bachmann for its 'Spectrum' range, which apart from Shay and Climax logging locomotives includes this splendid 'American type' 4-4-0.

Opposite, lower: Ample space and funds are needed to contemplate five-inch gauge garden railways, but this giant among scales has many devotees. Thomas, a Baldwin 2-6-2T, is electrically driven by the motor from a C5, the batteries being housed in the van permanently coupled to the engine.

This page: Rapt attention! A gathering of 16mm Scale enthusiasts – young and old – at a club meet.

1 Getting Started

Happiness is a garden railway!
Opposite, top: Graham
Powell enjoys a running
session on his Gauge 0 line,
built on a base of breeze
blocks banked by earth and turf.

Lower: Members of the
Gauge 3 Scenic Garden
Railway Society gather in
Dorset. The superb layout
depicts a terminus based
on Holyhead with the Irish
boat train awaiting departure.

This page: Just as it should
be – father plans and children
play. David Pratt considers
future developments on his
G Scale line.

You've decided that you are going to enter the world of outdoor model railways – Welcome! So where do you go from here? This book seeks to answer your questions in an organised and structured way, with just a few diversions here and there.

At the risk of stating the obvious, the first and most important point to bear in mind is not to let the hobby take over to the point where it ceases to be fun. Each one of us has his or her preferences. Engineering works in the garden of the family home can of course affect the whole family. Much nicer to involve the whole family, accommodating their individual interests, whether horticultural or construction.

The whole of this book is not, generally speaking, going to tell you to do anything, except when it come to safety aspects. The aim is to feed you with ideas, so that you are stimulated into making choices which suit the way that YOU want to go with YOUR railway, and to develop it to suit your own style and need. We are however, going to concentrate on what have become known as the 'Scenic Scales' – G Scale and 16mm or Gauge 1 – and on lines integrated with the garden.

A BEGINNING – MINIMUM REQIREMENTS

The absolute minimum is not much more than described above. You will

A tram or railcar can suffice as initial motive power on a basic garden railway.

need some track, something to run on it, and a power unit to make it all work. Of course, you will be itching to see the train running. At an early stage you should decide what style of layout you are going to build. Layout designs are discussed in a later section, but you should plan so that your initial trackwork can be put down fairly quickly, in such a way that running can commence and maintain your interest – and those around you! Yet you need to consider how the layout will develop as time and money permit, unlike the railroader who spent two years laying track without a wheel turning – then lost interest.

We would suggest initially either an end-to-end line, or a simple circuit. This will be influenced by the shape of your garden , and how the various features such as lawns, rockeries, or flower beds already make up the basic skeleton of its structure.

If you opt for end-to-end, then remember that you will be constantly stopping and starting the train, unless the line is long. Being your own engine driver may be fun to start with, and we know of a number of railway modellers who love shunting operations, but you might tire of it eventually. However, there is an advantage with this type of layout, in that it will impinge less on the existing framework of the garden, especially with a line laid alongside existing paths, lawns, or flower beds. There are automatic reversing units, some built into buffers, and these will be described later.

If you want things really simple, then all you need initially for motive power is a tram or a railcar. These need no wagons or carriages to haul, and so do not need points for running around at terminals, although sidings will be needed with your next rolling stock purchases.

Opting for a circular, or rather a continuous layout, will probably make more demands on your creative ability to integrate the railway into existing or planned garden features. A continuous run does have advantages though, because it allows you to start up a train and just let it run while you relax, watch it and plan the next development – or possibly even do some gardening!

If all this sounds rather basic, the scenic scales are of such a size and presence that once you get out of doors into the sunlight, then no matter how simple the layout or how limited the rolling stock, it looks real, just like the prototype. Which leads us on to...

The Real Thing

Models of narrow gauge railways can offer you the world, because the prototypes have so much variety. A train can consist of a single railcar, a steam, diesel or electric locomotive pulling or pushing one or two coaches with perhaps a van at the back for parcels or freight. At the other end of the spectrum we can have modern locomotives hauling a dozen or so coaches or wagons. The permutations are endless. There are in existence around the world narrow gauge systems with the latest technology, electric locomotives and all the panoply of a mainline system which rival the very best that standard gauge may have to offer. Equally there are ancient steam locomotives, weed covered track, rickety railbuses or hybrid systems that start off as tramways and end up as country branch lines.

Curiously, one of the least modelled times, yet perhaps the most interesting, was the time of the demise of steam and introduction of diesel and electric

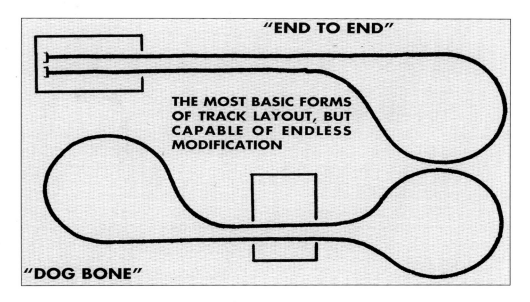

"END TO END"

THE MOST BASIC FORMS OF TRACK LAYOUT, BUT CAPABLE OF ENDLESS MODIFICATION

"DOG BONE"

Top: For the instant garden railway all that is needed is a flat area of grass, a spell of fine weather and a box of old Hornby tinplate track. An amazingly effective result can be obtained by using galvanised nails to hold the track firmly in place and mahogany strips under the sleepers to even out irregularities. A strimmer lightly run along the route will keep the grass from becoming too unruly.

Lower: The scenic scales are such that once you get outdoors, no matter how simple the layout, it looks real. This scene on the Longlands & Western Railway suggests sweeping vistas but in fact the line occupies a relatively small space.

traction. Even the latest European and Japanese 'High Speed Trains' which run at 200 or more kilometers an hour are available in the shops for our gauges.

This is the beauty of our scales. You will be able to chose the type of line that you want to run in your garden, and very likely be able to purchase ready-made models and accessories to suit. If you feel like creating your own models, a vast array of parts is available for 'scratchbuilding'. Or you can always modify that old Playmobil or Bachmann that got you started. There are brave modelers who modify LGB – despite the cost.

There is also great satisfaction in moulding a tunnel mouth in modelling clay, and casting this in quick setting cement via a latex mould, in the style of your particular railway.

KEEPING THE AUTHORITIES HAPPY

We have already mentioned that garden railways usually involve the whole family. They will not appreciate, however, a building site that has replaced their favourite piece of lawn or flower bed.

Ancient steam locomotives in far-flung parts of the world still potter along weed-ridden tracks and provide plenty of inspiration for garden railway enthusiasts. This particular example comes from a sugar line in Cuba built to the unlikely gauge of 2ft 4 1/2 inches.

Sweeping curves help a railway to blend in with and enhance the garden. A 4F 0-6-0 looks totally convincing as it trundles along Jack Ray's long-established Gauge 0 Crewchester line.

Ground level lines do suffer from the wildlife – snails and insects use them as freeways through the undergrowth – with fatal results. Rain and frost can bring higher maintenance with a need to keep points free of debris thrown around by pecking birds. The viewpoint for observing your railway is alos far too high and unrealistic. Looking down from 45degress two or three feet to six feet away is best.

A garden railway should blend in with and enhance the garden, just as a pond or fountain already does. There should be a reason for the tunnel or bridge in maintaining a level track despite the ups and downs of the terrain. Not only does this make the whole garden more pleasing to the eye but helps to create a more realistic appearance. It will also draw other members of your family into taking an interest. While you are planning or building with a railwayman's eye, your partners can most certainly help and advise independently about gardening aspects.

Many happy hours can be spent at gardening centres, choosing suitable heathers, ground cover plants, alpines, or dwarf conifers to complement the railway. It is possible to make the whole of the lineside a herb garden, since most of these plants have small leaves and flowers in scale with the passing trains. Watching plants mature over the years as the railway also slowly develops is a most satisfying part of the hobby.

When you are planning your line, and assuming you are to have conventional electric model powered traction, you can certainly allow for some gradients, but we suggest nothing steeper than one in forty. Many models have a rubber traction tyre on a wheel to assist with on gradients. All locomotives rely on their weight for a grip in real life. Allowing for some gradients, and the need for a bridge or tunnel to add variety, you should be able to follow the contours that exist.

The best angle from which to view your railway, we have said, is about two feet above, with a lineside view now and then, following our real life view at stations or perhaps over a linside fence. It is clearly impossible for most people to have their railways naturally elevated to three or four feet above the ground, and so compromises are required.

If your garden is more or less level, then some gentle gradients will add interest to the running. They will also make live steam engines work harder and so sound better. Often it is possible to dig a hole for a pond, and use the spoil for an embankment, though grass cutting could be a problem. Camomile looks the part and covers the ground like moss.

Track construction and laying are covered elsewhere in this book, but bear in mind that firm foundations are vital. This is engineering for real! Try to avoid laying the track in dead straight lines, but instead follow gentle curves, complementing the shapes existing in the garden, or creating new ones for the railway. Prototype narrow gauge lines are pretty sinuous anyway. The reason for the narrow gauge is to allow sharper curves. After all, narrow gauge came about because of its flexibility in coping with gradients, curves and dramatic landscape changes. Main lines were built for the fastest route between two cities.

A train will look more interesting if it is allowed to wind through the garden environment with light and shadow falling at different angles on locomotive and rolling stock.

Motive Power

Here we are talking about the method of propulsion for your models. In large-scale model railways you do have some choice in the matter, although the vast majority of G Scale modellers use electric power. That is, the mains feeding a transformer, with the trains drawing up to twenty volts and more than two amps from the rails. This is a very reliable method, particularly over large

Means of motive power.
Above: Electric power through the rails is used by the vast majority of G Scale modellers. This LGB 0-4-4-0 Meyer has a smoke generator, directional lighting and a motor in each drive unit – giving tremendous haulage potential.

Opposite, top: Accucraft's 1:20.3 scale Rio Grande Southern 'Galloping Goose'. A model of this kind offers ample space for conversion to battery power.
Lower: Not quite what it seems. This LGB 0-6-6-0 Mallet is drawing its power from batteries concealed in the bogie van behind the locomotive. A lead from the van is plugged into the lighting socket, which is a feature of virtually all LGB models.

distances and if the pieces of track are bonded together electrically to reduce voltage drop and 'dead' track. However, you must contrive to keep any mains cable indoors, and preferably with a sensitive circuit breaker at the live end. Some of the latest developments by major manufacturers allow for independent control of a number of trains on the same track, and also for setting points from a central controller.

If you have power supplied to the track continuously, and begin to run more than one locomotive, it may be advantageous to provide isolating sections, where you can switch off the track electricity. This will allow trains to be 'parked', at a station or siding for instance, while others are run. Many locomotives actually have a switch, whereby you can turn off the power to the wheels, leaving the lights or smoke generator operating, or combinations of these.

Another form of motive power supply is the good old battery, rechargeable or otherwise. Some locomotives, particularly diesels, are bulky enough to accept a pack of Ni-Cad rechargeables, or even lead-acid moped/scooter batteries and a small controller operated by radio. Pushed to the limit, you can even find space for the electronic digital sound generator, and loudspeaker too! Alternatively, these can all be located in a goods van immediately behind the locomotive.

Most models are weatherproof, and to cater for masochists there are even snow-ploughs on the market to keep your railway running in the most severe conditions!

The prudent railway builder will also allow for the possibility of real steam and larger locomotives – even multiples – American style. This can affect the radii of curves, which are generally less than those that can be negotiated by traction motor bogies.

Finally, make sure that you can expand the layout, if and when required. There is also the possibility of moving house. The construction methods suggested in this book also allow for alteration, growth and ultimate removal of the railway. The 'permanent way' can be less than permanent and the ground easily re-instated, even after some years of use and enjoyment.

A simple design often gives pleasing results. The Baldwin tank waits at a junction for the passenger train to come past.

2
Planning the Railway

Devising the plan is probably the most important activity of all. Hours, weeks and months spent on planning and designing a garden railway will always be well rewarded. The potential problems go far beyond those of an indoor layout in smaller scales, where it can be merely the case of seeing that curves and points will fit into the space available. Outside, the frequent absence of any specific boundaries can make the number of possibilities so numerous that sometimes the newcomer simply does not know where to begin.

There is a great responsibility in the fact that you are creating something semi-permanent at least, and changing the real environment, so be sure that you are doing so for the better. Try in the first instance to take an overall view and decide which type of line will give the greatest satisfaction, not just to yourself but to the whole household. Garden railways used to be an all male preserve, but this is no longer the case. The modern concept involves a line which, by careful planning and planting, provides a natural setting for the railway, and enhances rather than disfigures the surroundings of flower beds, lawns or rockery. Finally, make sure that you can develop the layout in the future.

PROTOTYPE OR FREELANCE?

Although the great outdoors might at first glance seem ideal to model a prototype station or section of a real line, this is much harder than it seems. The sheer size of our models means that an enormous space is required, and usually something gets in the way. Any slight departure from the real thing will defeat the object of the exercise, and so most modellers opt for a 'freelance' or 'fun' railway. This can take on any form depending on the personality of the operator.

Driver, signalman or constructor? Are you the sort of entusiast who in imagination is firmly in the cab of a locomotive, following it round the tracks as it constantly shunts and changes the train make-up (the consist). If so, a

layout with several stations, goods depots or sidings will be required. Others dream of being signalmen, directing trains to the appointed place on the line, or platform at the station. In this case junctions, loops and multiple routing possibilities are likely to be favoured.

Then again, the spectator who is happy to watch the trains go round will prefer a simple design, with broad sweeping curves. Lastly, but by no means least, there will be many who wish to give added interest as well as purpose to their gardening for gardeningís sake, providing an extra dimension to the rockery, alpines and dwarf planting, drawing together all the horticultural elements, giving them purpose.

LAYOUT CHARACTER

There are many options here. The simplest layout of all, the continuous circuit, can work quite satisfactorily in the garden, where plants and landscaping can quite easily disguise the circular nature. It is ideal for the spectator, and is also particularly useful for live-steam operation. A variant, especially on sloping ground, is the dumb-bell or dog-bone shape. Even these can be twisted upon themselves so that the track crosses over itself, giving the appearance of two passing railways.

An out-and-back system is easy for the single operator as well, although a relatively large space is needed for the turning circle. The 'driver' may prefer end-to-end operation with the two termini close together, if he is on his own

Opposite, top: A garden railway wholly integrated into its surroundings can give a wonderful sense of achievement. This view was taken in late evening sunshine on a G Scale line some 750ft up in the Pennines.

Lower: An elevated line can equally well blend into the garden by careful use of stonework and background planting. The Merseyside Express, double-headed by a 'Jumbo' and a Midland Compound, looks well on this Gauge 1 layout.

This page: Provision for stations and passing places needs to be considered during initial layout planning. Woodside on the Rainbow Valley Tramway is little more than a loop but is perfectly adequate for its purpose.

Basing the garden line on a specific location helps to give a sense of identity. The legendary 2ft gauge Darjeeling Himalayan Railway, with an average grade of 1 in 30 and some curves sharper than 50 feet radius, forms an inspiring but seldom modelled prototype. Dutch enthusiast Huub Brech has faithfully captured the lines of its Sharp Stewart tanks and four-wheeled rolling stock.

or space is limited. Separate termini are more authentic, for the trains have two places to connect by rail transport. They also give the greatest return in terms of train movements and types.

The 'signalmen' among us will favour a combination of two or more of the above, which is perfectly feasible, perhaps working from a central signal box – the garden shed- with an overview of the important parts if not all of the line.

As with an indoor layout, it helps if the line has a sense of purpose and credibility, an identity. Is it to be a main line carrying fast passenger and freight traffic, or a sleepy branch with mixed trains? Will it be in central Europe, the U.S.A., South Africa, Alaska? Will it be last century, the beginning of this, or more recent still? Then again, it could be industrial, serving a quarry or sawmill, and perhaps hauling real loads from one place to another.Or might it be more of a tramway, starting in a townscape and turning at the journey's end in a country setting?

Recently, there has been a resurgence of interest in Gauge 3 – standard gauge trains at the same scale as G Scale narrow gauge. There are now sufficient shop-available products and accessories to allow narrow gauge branch lines, industrial or otherwise, to meet with the main line (Gauge 3) at a junction station. The buildings and figures will be the same size for both.

For live steam, operating 'fire lighting' pits are needed, suitably drained, where fires and ash can be handled safely, and all parts of the locomotives, even underneath, can be attended to. Any excavated material goes to cover the area of a planned tunnel.

All of these considerations need careful thought, and only when firm

conclusions have been reached should detailed planning begin.

Your first job as Chief Civil Engineer of your railway will be to conduct a survey. This is exactly what Isambard Kingdom Brunel did when to walked the whole distance from Paddington to Bristol, before he built his Great Western Railway. You follow in mighty footsteps – with a long tape measure and squared paper! Take a reference point that is level, the damp course of a house, and try to give an indication of any general rise or fall in ground level over the whole site, say north-south and east-west.

Modern methods of track planning can involve computers and the Internet (www.winrail.com is one). There are several simple and inexpensive software design packages (template generators) that will assist 21st century railway builders.

The increasing availability of British-outline buildings permits the creation of townscapes, including Coronation Street style terrace houses with backyards.

A ROOF FOR ALL SEASONS

Many garden railways start off with a simple open-air line. The rolling stock is carried in and out for each operating session. Apart from the risk of damage from repeated handling, this can soon become a chore – and anyway, real railways do not work like this. It is far more satisfactory if the line can include a covered area which can keep the rolling stock dry when it rains or snows – railway personnel appreciate this consideration too. The undercover area can be part

of the house car port, or garage. Greenhouses should be avoided because of the huge temperature variations and high humidity.

Another possibility is a free-standing shed, sited near the house for security reasons and fed with a mains electricity supply, suitably fuse protected. This shed may have to be sizeable. Scale trains can be up to fifteen feet long – and more if they emulate U.S. freight practice.

Local Authority regulations have to be observed for a permanent brick built structure, which might be included as part of any house development. Certainly those contemplating five-inch lines will need to be careful about drawing attention to the works and operations. In any event, doors, windows and any train hatches must all be lockable. The shed can combine both termini of any end-to-end line or be in the centre of a dog-bone layout. It can also provide a site office during construction ñ somewhere to solder, and make the tea.

With a decision on the concept and type of line, its position in the garden, and the most suitable home for the rolling stock, actual layout planning can now begin in detail. Start by making your sketches on paper. Keep it simple and, assuming that this is the more usual freelance line, remember that you are aiming for some fun and enjoyment rather than authenticity. The more extensive it is, the more it will cost to build and to maintain. Single track will be cheaper by half of course, and also gives a better illusion of distance.

Allow for future expansion and branches. In devising the track plan there must be sufficient provision for shunting, and for trains to pass each other, as well as stabling spare locomotives and rolling stock. Run-round loops should be long enough for the longest trains that you can foresee. The locomotive needs to be able to move from front to rear of the train for its return journey. Buildings can take up a great deal of space, and then there is the planting. Often, with larger layouts, it is a good idea to install 'set pieces', such as a quarry, docks, village, main station, where activity can be concentrated.

Opposite, top: Running the line into a covered area avoids the chore of carrying the rolling stock outside for each operating session. An A-B-A set of LGB F7s, in striking Santa Fe livery, emerges into the great outdoors and crosses a steel trestle to reach ground level.

Lower: Hauling loads – real or imaginary – from one place to another adds interest to garden railway operations. An LGB 2-6-0T is shunting at a quarry screening plant before taking the 'processed stone' off to the main terminus.

This page: Plans have been completed and construction work is well in hand on a major 'above ground' terminus.

Tunnels are a wonderful feature, but Murphy's law dictates that disasters will always occur in their most inaccessible reaches. This American layout uses the correct wooden-faced tunnel mouth.

At an early stage you need to decide upon the locations of tunnels and bridges, cuttings and embankments, especially if they are forced upon you by the garden's topography. Tunnels should be viewed with great caution. Murphy's law dictates that if something can go wrong, then it will do so in a tunnel. Any tunnel must be readily accessible, with the centre within arm's reach.

When it comes to crossing pathways, ground level is preferable to a lifting section in an elevated track. 'Bar flaps', sometimes disguised as a bridge that will lift out or hinge up, always require some clever electrical connections and security measures to avoid spectators lifting track in the path of an oncoming train.

Cuttings too have their drawbacks, being damp and prone to landslips with difficult tracklaying and maintenance. They are also a collecting area for fallen leaves and windblown rubbish. They are especially valued by animals as footpaths. There are garden suction cleaners for removing leaves – these work well for general track-clearing duties.

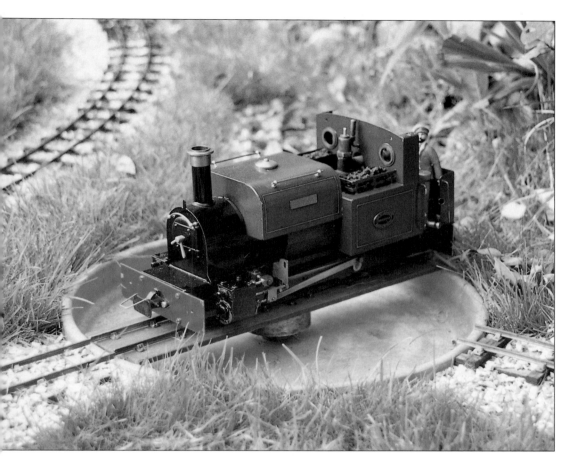

A turntable can be a useful feature, especially on end-to-end layouts. This one is based on a terra cotta saucer purchased for less than £5 from a specialist retailer.

Curves and gradients are a key factor in your trackwork and also in enhancing realism. Those with indoor layouts will have to adjust from minimum radius thinking to always providing maximum available radius on curves. Think big! Try to use 'transitional curves' – a shallower curve. on entering a sharper one. This follows prototypical practice. Long sweeping curves give the best views of trains in motion.

Flexible tracks a great advantage and also a saving over sectional track with its pre-formed curves and short straights. It also give fewer joints to bond with up to five foot lengths.

Similarly, nothing looks worse than sharp radius turnouts (points) when there is all the space in the world, and long wagons or locomotives are forced to overhang unrealistically or dangerously. There is always a temptation to use small radius points and components on cost grounds but you will almost always want to change to larger radius as your operational experience grows.

Remember, friction will be increased if a locomotive, already working hard uphill, runs into a curve and the flanges begin to bite against the inside of the rails. Experienced steam locomotive drivers, starting a heavy train on a curve, will back up first, easing the couplings. This means that the locomotive takes up the weight and strain one carriage or wagon at a time and wheel slip is avoided.

Many of the same principles apply to gradients. The desirable maximum gradient is about one in sixty for live steam, and one in thirty for electric traction. With the latter, short trains, hauled by a heavy engine (for better traction through its greater adhesion) can cope with one in twenty five for short lengths, but this only increases wear on tracks and locomotives. This wear was also very common on main lines with real locomotives suffering from broken springs and worn bearings. Gradients should be the vertical equivalent of transitional curves, with a more gentle gradient leading to the incline proper. A severe incline in the middle of a curve is an engine driver's nightmare!

SURVEYING

After drawing and redrawing many plans on paper, the time will come to translate into reality on the ground. Some modellers lay the track in position on mother earth, and start digging. A more exact approach is usually preferable, particularly if you are opting for more permanent foundations. A combination of boards, stakes, spirit level, and string is needed. A very useful device for levelling over large distances is a garden hose with a length of clear tubing attached to each end. When this is filled with water, wherever the two ends are, the visible water level in them will be the same – a fact unknown to the Romans it seems.

Straight and level track laying is easy enough. Simply lay a board on the ground and place a spirit level on top, excavating and filling until the desired

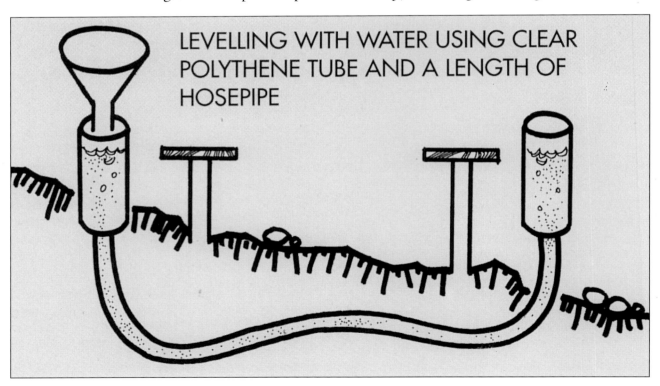

LEVELLING WITH WATER USING CLEAR POLYTHENE TUBE AND A LENGTH OF HOSEPIPE

result is obtained. The 'spoil' surplus is used to fill in hollows just as the 'navvies' built the nineteenth century's vast railway networks. You are still following that long and honourable tradition.

Gradients require a little calculation. If a board a hundred units long is raised by one unit at the end, you have a gradient of one in a hundred. Curves are measured by driving a stake into the ground at the centrepoint of the desired curve. Attach a length of string, and 'draw' your giant circle just as you would with a compass – with a trickle of sand.

Realism through gradual curvature on a 16mm Scale line near Oban. The locomotive is home-built using a 7 amp motor and two motor-cycle batteries – and has no trouble coping with a 60-axle load.

3
Trackwork and Bases

Perhaps the largest expense at the beginning of your railway project will be the track itself. It is impossible to build a railway a metre at a time, so you must complete a section at one go. This will also assist with your electrical isolation and supplies later on. There are many types of track available from many manufacturers. In G Scale the 45mm gauge track can be divided into three types;

(a) Track completely compatible with LGB, such as Bachmann, REA/Aristo, Lionel. Playmobil is indistinguishable form LGB.
(b) Track that is compatible with special joiners – Tenmille G Scale, Peco G Scale.
(c) Track that will not join to LGB because of totally different rail and sleeper sections/measurements, e.g. Tenmille Gauge One.

Lehmann (LGB) offers a very comprehensive track system, based upon sectional and flexible long length types. All rails are solid brass (expensive) with weather resistant plastic sleepers fully detailed with chairs and woodgrain. This base is manufactured from BASF Luran-S for good sunlight stability and frost resistance. You can stand on it without harm.

Rail joiners are brass or yellow insulating plastic. Apart from the vast catalogue of pre-formed track sections, there are train detecting switches or magnets, diamond crossings and various points layouts. Flexible lengths of 1.5 metres are most useful.

Points (turnouts to railwaymen) are available from LGB in two radii. The smaller circle is sold by Playmobil at a slightly lower price through toy shops. Lehmann recently introduced a budget 'Toy Train' label. Some specialist suppliers – such as Garden Railway Specialists (U.K. Internet mail order) – also supply very long and large radius point work, and 'specials' to order. These have treated wooden sleepers. Larger radius turnouts are always worth the extra investment. All types can be operated by electric motors in weatherproof housings which also accept switch attachments and direction lanterns, and in

Just a few of the many varieties of Gauge 1 (45mm) track. Left to right: Dual gauge Gargraves track with hollow stainless steel rail; flat bottom track built to 16mm scale; Gauge 1 Model Railway Association rail and components used to make 10mm scale bullhead track; flat bottom turnout with moving frog.

some cases operate signals as well.

The large range of track accessories includes uncouplers, manual and remotely operated, and tipping wagon activators.

Other major players in our hobby, such as Bachmann, offer trackwork, in metal with metal sleepers, and all plastic. The major U.K. manufacturers are Tenmille and Peco, both widely available or direct. Peco G45 track has irregular sleepers and so more closely resembles much of the narrow gauge trackwork. Aluminium rail is also availbale but is not really suited to a wetter climate because of the peculiar oxidation.

Track, usually designed for Gauge 1, has sleeper spacing more in keeping with U.K. mainline standards, with wood or plastic sleepers. Chairs for wooden sleepers are usually plastic, with a small spigot that pushes into a small hole drilled into the sleeper. Rail profiles can be 'flat-bottomed' or 'bullhead'. The use of such finely modelled trackwork usually puts restrictions on the laying, and also operation of rolling stock. The effect of modelling mainline can be very realistic – especially with an Aster Japanese model of the Mallard A4 live steam moving past.

The main problem with running on different manufacturers' tracks with different rolling stock is the continuous changes over time that are made to running gear. Wheel flanges are made larger or smaller, or 'frogs' on points have less clearance. The motto is be careful when you see a bargain that was produced some or many years ago, and your track is recent.

As mentioned above, certain provisos attach to the use of 10mm scale track systems such as Tenmille products. Modern LGB products will run successfully on this track. However since LGB appeared in the 1960s there have been at least three sizes of wheel flange. Many wheels are also from very hard brass, making replacement the best option. The problems of derailment are mostly caused by flanges and clearances on pointwork.

TRACK BASES

Second only in importance to the selection and planning of the tracks is the decision on the type of track base necessary to carry your railway. There are many kinds of track, and each and every railway has its own pet idea and favourite system or manufacturers. We can therefore only hope to offer a sampling from the more common developments that have taken place in the recent growth of the hobby.

The simplest base will probably be a patio or terrace. Many people have laid railways in such places, but unless the patio is reasonably large, and the railway integrated in some fashion, you will simply be operating a train set, not building a railway. Even the boxed starter railway sets assume some degree of permanence.

Trench technique track base of polythene filled with pea gravel and bricks

'Post on end' to track height and earth embankment or viaduct between

The aim of this book, after all, is to show how easily and enjoyably one can build a more permanent railway into or around the garden environs. By all means run the tracks via a patio or conservatory – perhaps on a two foot high wooden trestle? The railway, we keep emphasising, should enhance the garden with movement and added interest.

Probably the simplest method of forming a track base is to dig a trench in the ground some four inches deep, sprinkling some weed killer into the bottom – beware of nearby growing plant roots, then line the trench with polythene sheet, holes punched at random for drainage. Fill the trench back to ground level with loose (sharp) chipings, which lock in place and form a stable yet water friendly foundation for everything above. Smaller than 5-6mm or round ballast is not so stable and can wander all over the garden. The trough sides can be made of treated wood, metal, or fancy lawn edging

Tracks can be laid directly, five inch tracks almost always are. Skewers straight down into the ground hold tracks in place in simple fashion. Clearly this work is all reversible.

A better method is to insert bricks or soft blocks into the ballast, then wriggle them to the correct height with your board and spirit level. Brass screws can go straight into the blocks, or into plugs in bricks. In more stable ground conditions, soft insulating blocks can be let into the ground on their sides making a flat and level surface for trackwork. Hardwood blocks in concrete have been used. Drainage and frost will shorten their life however.

Track base formed of hardcore laid between bricks. The top two to three inches are pea shingle on top of a layer of sand. Notice the point already in place for future extensions.

Concrete is a more permanent base, and is particularly useful in station areas, which will be much wider, level places. A quick mix of concrete can be shovelled and spread to rough level, then trowelled or scraped with the board, even onto the ballast base. Hard concrete blocks , which are not prone to water or frost damage, work well at ground level. A thin layer of ballast can be overlaid and track fixed with brass screws and plugs. Screws should not project above sleeper height, and nothing at all can project above rail height!

Recent earthworks should always be left for a while to let the elements compact the surface material before any engineering or laying of trackwork takes place.

External grade PVA glue works well for fixing small track ballast in place, then grass cutting near the track with strimmers and 'garden-vac' equipment is assisted.

A well laid track, screwed down where strength is required, held as a curve by 'Plastic Padding' (automotive filler), and PVA plus fish tank gravel for ballast, will remain in place for some years, then be reasonably easy to remove.

Experienced gardeners will know that if cement and peat are mixed with sand, you have produced 'Hypatufa' – a sort of natural rock – which will mellow and grow green algae or moss quite quickly. This material is used to form artificial rocks, by digging an irregular hole in the ground, and filling it

Opposite: Stages in the construction of a terminus designed to give a comfortable operating height.

Top, left: Completing the base, which consumed over four tons of hardcore.

Top, right: With the base consolidated, concrete has been laid and track-laying can begin.

Lower: Ballasting in progress, using a mix of fish-tank gravel and quick setting mortar which is brushed into place.

This page: Many garden railways still use traditional track bases formed of timber resting on treated wooden posts.

with chicken wire and 'Hypatufa'. After a few days the 'rock' can be pulled up from the ground and used for railway purposes.

A somewhat older method of forming track bases, and still common with some live steam modelling, where the train representing years of work is important, is to use well seasoned and preserved timber. Be careful, some model sleeper plastics are sensitive to 'Creosote' preservatives. Building sites have often proved to be useful sources of old or suitably sized timbers. A single Gauge 1, Gauge 3, or G Scale track needs a width of about six inches for its track base, and possibly wider on sharp curves to allow for rolling stock 'overhang'.

Many garden railways are built on a base of short, treated ('tanalised') three and a half inch fence-posts sunk into the ground, or dry mix concrete, then decked with five inch timber planks ñ such as 'scaffold' boards. If this is just to raise track two feet or so then earth can be used to infill under the track level to produce an 'embankment'. Alternatively, small leaved Privet hedging can be planted under the timber deck. Metal or thin wood/plastic strips can be used to form an edging. This will retain derailed trains and ballast.

Where the railway crosses a path or other level outdoor base, an ideal track fixing material is 2mm fish tank gravel, mixed with quick setting mortar, then funnelled around sleepers and left overnight to set and harden. 5mm granite chips look best around Gauge 1 and larger, when trach is laid directly onto a trough of larger ballast or 'pea-gravel'. Both can be bought in bags from garden centres, which will also deliver larger quantities of all these materials for those with the most ambitious plans.

To follow a curve at ground level, with the trough method, then more bricks or blocks are used and wooden sections need to be shortened. This system facilitates possible relocation and additions. In our experience, a life of five years is to be expected.

With a considerable investment in time and money fixed to the ground, the re-usability of trackwork is a consideration. Garden scales are inherently much stronger than smaller scales, and take moving and relaying in their stride.

A final note – if you have the time, make the foundations for the track a season before you commence your engineering work to let everything settle. You might also see where wild animals have runs, squirrels dig for hidden nuts, flooded areas need some drainage, and leaves are blown into rotting piles. It pays to do your planning one year, commence work in autumn, then start on the planned railway the following spring.

RACK RAILWAYS (ROCKERIES)

These railways are found all over mountainous country, for example in Switzerland, India, and Wales. They are basically a cog-wheel meshing with a toothed centre rail in the tracks. Everyday railways rely on friction caused by the adhesion weight of the locomotive, and its number of driving wheels, for tractive effort. A 4-6-2 express locomotive might weigh a hundred and forty

tons with about eighteen tons on each wheel for adhesion and traction. Where steep grades occur, physical factors limit the amount of friction available. Sometimes sand is sprayed under the driving wheels to improve grip, but at enormous cost to the life of the railway's equipment. To overcome these problems on steep grades, a system was developed which transferred the power of the locomotive directly to the cog running on the toothed rail, fixed firmly to the embedded sleepers.

On the rack! The LGB Schollenen Railway locomotive climbs steeply up a rockery. A cog wheel engages with a plastic centre toothed rail to give adhesion on gradients as steep as 1 in 4.

LGB is the only manufacturer so far to offer a modelling system for a rack railway that can climb a rockery. The plastic centre toothed rail is available in 300mm lengths, and is fixed to ordinary tracks with special clips, which locate between the sleepers. Installation and removal is very easy, and does not affect regular trains on the same tracks.

LGB also make a cable car system that can be set to run from the base to the top of your planned rockery, to meet up at the 'Summit' station with the rack railway. Preiser and others will provide the skis and figures to populate your ski resort.

If you are planning to provide a rack railway to the top of your rockery, winding among the rocky outcrops and passing through tunnels and over gorges on the way, please note that lumps of rock from garden centres can cost ten times a large load ordered straight from a quarry. Quarries will usually deliver a part load, on their way to the garden centre, of half to one hundred-weight pieces, giving twenty to forty pieces to the ton. Two to four tons should start you off!

To help your planning – the LGB rack locomotives are capable of climbing a maximum grade of one in four (e.g. a rise of 25 units for every 100 units travelled). A somewhat lesser grade is more usual in real life however. It is also wise to remember that sharp curves impart more friction.

When laying track it is best to use the longest, flexible type, particularly at the entrance and exit to the gradient or changes to the slope. It is extremely difficult to bend shorter sectioned track in the vertical direction. These also do not look the part.

One of the most common problems often encountered at the commencement of gradients is that rolling stock will uncouple. LGB make a coupling with a smaller arm so that fouling of the rack is avoided. They also recommend for the safety of your passengers that hooks are fitted at both ends of the carriages to avoid that most dreadful of events ñ a runaway carriage or wagon careering down a mountainside!

Track-laying – and wiring
– in progress on a G Scale
layout.

4
Electrics and Electronics

Opposite: Electric power in the garden.

Top: Hartland Locomotive Works 4-4-0 running on scale track.

Lower: An LGB layout, with a 0-6-6-0 Mallet awaiting its next turn of duty in the foreground. Buildings are by Pola.

This page: Soldering outdoors, necessary when bonding track joints, requires clean rails and ideally a gas-powered blowlamp with a large heat-sink bit attached. Care is needed to avoid damage to plastic sleepers.

Now that we have a clearer idea of the work involved in trackwork and track bases – the infrastructure on which our railway will rest – the next logical step is to turn to electrics, for most of the model railways in the world, and this applies in the garden too, are electrically powered.

Ultimately, the power will come from the mains. This is a potentially dangerous, even lethal adjunct to our railway, and we must take care. Mains power is best brought to a building such as your ëtrain shedí, and the staff and onlookers further protected by quick blow sensitive fuses (circuit breakers) of the earth leakage type. These blow easily at small overloads, or if an electrical short occurs. Good practice also suggests that you fit an on/off isolating switch at the incoming supply point to disconnect everything in an emergency or for maintenance. A good precaution is to hang a 'DANGER' label on this switch if you are working on the electrics somewhere out of sight, and tell someone that this is where you are.

TRACK ELECTRICAL SUPPLY

It is worth repeating at this stage the earlier mentioned

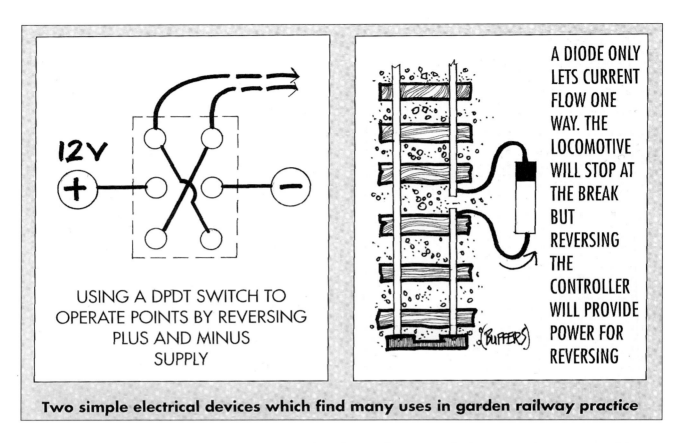

12V

USING A DPDT SWITCH TO
OPERATE POINTS BY REVERSING
PLUS AND MINUS
SUPPLY

A DIODE ONLY
LETS CURRENT
FLOW ONE
WAY. THE
LOCOMOTIVE
WILL STOP AT
THE BREAK
BUT
REVERSING
THE
CONTROLLER
WILL PROVIDE
POWER FOR
REVERSING

(BUFFERS)

Two simple electrical devices which find many uses in garden railway practice

maxim – Keep it Simple! This applies particularly to any electrics out of doors. The more complicated the system, the more faults can occur, and the harder they are to trace. There is also more maintenance and consequently less train running.

Again, at the risk of repetition, plan your electrical requirements. Decide where you need section breaks and isolating joins in the rails. Playmobil make a very simple trackside weatherproof isolating switch. In the real world, a train passes from block to block and is handed from signal box to signal box. You might start with a similar plan. In our garden railway world we also have to be able to park a train, and switch off its power while we attend to another activity. The siting of block isolating switches in a signal box (or garden shed) should be carefully planned. It is far better to have all your switches protected from the elements, even if they are outdoor specified types. At least there is less risk of corrosion.

The low voltage power supply input to the track should still use the heaviest cable possible, even mains house-wiring cable. The reason for this is simple – voltage drop, a phenomenon that is especially prevalent in garden railways with their long distances at low voltages. A ten metre run of 1mm cable can lose nearly two volts. Usually 18 to 22 volts are needed at the farthest point from the supply, whether a controller or simple direct feed to the track for radio controlled trains. Motors usually require 1.5 amps; the better quality the motor, the less the current drain. A locomotive with two motors, sound

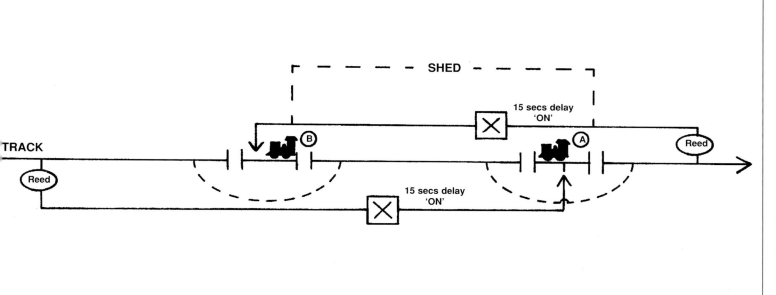

generating module, smoke generator, coach lighting and a heavy train will draw over 5 amps.

Depending upon your isolating sections, your feed should be out along the track whenever possible. A heavy-section brass rail has greater current carrying capacity and larger cross section than any 5 amp mains cable. In order to use the track supply successfully, it is vital to bond all rail joints for electrical circuit continuity – except where you want a break. This usually means soldering a jumper wire across each joint, a single copper wire from a 5 amp housewiring cable cut into short lengths. Under no circumstances should the fishplates be soldered to the rails; no expansion in warm weather, or contraction in winter could occur, and buckling or displacement will result. If you look at the fishplates on real railway track you will see that they are greased to allow for movement of each individual piece. The rails are also electrically bonded with wire for train detection.

Most garden railways use an 18 to 22 volt track supply, with varying currents from 1 to 10 amps. This in turn requires some large transformers to drop the mains voltage, and powerful controllers, capable of handling currents that can on occasion give a mild shock.

Because we are usually dealing with the same low voltages as we find in motor cars and motor cycle electrics and components, there are many items that we may find useful, readily available, reliable and cheap. For instance, the copper filled grease for disc brakes can be used in fishplate rail joints to ensure electrical connection, and can be as good as a soldered wire. A battery charger delivering 12 volts 8 amps will run quite a number of 'interior' festoon light bulbs in railway buildings and sidings, thus enhancing your sunset running.

A simple automatic way to run two trains on one track, halving the wear and doubling the interest. One train stops and the other runs for one circuit. The delay is only to allow the loco enough time to start and clear the "dead" track. An automotive unit, for switching car interior lights, can be used.

Cleaning the rails.

Top: LGB's track cleaning locomotive, fitted with abrasive pads that revolve in the opposite direction to travel and thus grind the rail surface.

Lower: An adapted squeegee mop being used to good effect on a line in Denver, Colorado.

Delay modules that switch off your car's interior lights after you leave it are useful for automatic station stops and running two trains on the same track alternately. For commercial railways this can halve the wear on wheels and motors.

The size of the power supply will depend very much on the size of the locomotive(s), number of electric traction motors, size of train, and the gradients of the line. Nowadays it is possible to have a radio controlled throttle – a radio-interfaced central controller, which will allow you to control trains remotely while you wander around the garden. This system allows maximum flexibility of working and does away with the need for long leads with controllers on the end. Power supplies for any of these systems should be indoors with only the radio controller unit(s) outside.

Soldering outdoors requires a large soldering iron, clean track, and perhaps a warm day. A gas powered blowlamp with a large heat-sink soldering bit attached is best. Done carefully, the plastic sleepers will not melt, but use a piece of metal as a heat shield if possible. The simplest way to start is to solder

Overhead wires give a whole new perspective to a garden railway. They also cope well with extreme weather conditions!

a wire to each end of the rails before the track leaves the workshop. At a later stage during laying, the leads can be attached to adjacent rails or used for power feeds. Track with no bonding leaves the fishplates solely for electrical coductivity, yet they will corrode, fill with dirt and generally fail in the end.

Clever devices have been offered on the market, particularly in the USA, in an effort to get around this problem. They often consist of a clamp over the rail joiner and two set screws which clamp metal to metal. REA/Aristo offer track with two screws already at the joint.

LGB make a track cleaning locomotive , hand held scraper blocks, and sprung abrasive pads to fit under a wagon, all to wage the rail cleaning war for you. However, once this is accomplished all kinds of possibilities open up. But if your entire railway lies under trees that drip sticky juice, pine needles or sycamore seeds, there is another answer awaiting you.

We will look at on-board battery power in the next section. There are manually set control units which will slow to a stop or speed up a locomotive, deriving power from rechargeable batteries or a small scooter battery ñ which will run a train all day.

Putting electronics in a garden setting usually means disaster. Leaving units in a wooden garden shed over the winter is not a good idea. Any building should be wind proof, insulated, and possibly with low temperature greenhouse heating left on all winter – but do not allow wild life an entry!

OVERHEAD WIRES FOR POWER SUPPLY

Catenary is the commonly used term for overhead wiring that supplies electric current to trams and trains, although the word catenary strictly applies to the supporting wires from which the contact wire is suspended to form a level contact surface. The masts are usually made of treated (zinc plated) steel but can be concrete or timber. Attached to these masts are metal arms hanging out over the track, and the support cable (catenary) is strung between these, curving down in the centre of each gap centrally along the track. The contact wire is hung from the catenary wire by insulators and the last component here is short 'dropper' wires spaced along the length of the cable.

There are several types of catenary. We will concern ourselves only with the simple system described above and used on many electrified railway and tram systems. The variation called 'trolley wire' is used primarily on tramways where the masts can be close enough together to prevent serious sagging of the contact wire, and speeds are low. There is no 'catenary' suspension cable between the mast arms.

G Scale modellers are fortunate again, as LGB have produced both catenary and trolley wire systems. Other manufacturers are beginning to offer trams and rolling stock as well. It has to be said that LGB catenary is an expensive system but it does look very real. The aluminium masts clip to the track. There are two support arms – for the catenary and contact wires. A special version of the mast is available with a swivel base to keep it vertical on the steep gradients of a rockery rack railway. By a lucky accident, 'Double-O' scale rails are perfect for contact 'wire' in G Scale catenary practice.

The view – of masts, finely detailed locomotives, some like the 'Crocodile' of impressive size, with current collecting pantographs that move up and down upon change of direction – is perhaps one of the nearest to reality that garden railways can provide. There are very modern overhead pick up models on the market.

Simple catenary, using LGB masts and upside-down Peco 00 nikel-silver rail supported by brass wire.

5
Radio and Remote Control

Opposite, top: Radio control equipment has gradually become more compact, as instanced by the transmitter seen in the foreground of this picture. A locomotive like LGB's Nikki + Frank S is ideal for conversion to radio control, the tender giving adequate space for the batteries, servos and receiver.

Lower: This open cab shows the neat arrangement of servos and fittings that is possible on a live steam locomotive. The wires leading to the servos, fasted to the cab back, can clearly be seen. Atlantic is a John Shawe coal-fired version of a Roundhouse 'Argyll', based on a Campbeltown & Machrihanish Railway 0-6-2T.

This page: A young enthusiast tests an early product of Merlin Locomotive Works. Oil, water syringe and matches are at the ready, and the radio transmitter is being held at the correct angle – more-or-less!

When we have established our permanent way and become more confident in 'driving' our locomotive, or now have more than one, we may find it worthwhile to take a closer look at the way we control operations.

Real railway practice will invade a great deal of our train running, even when fun is the object, and usually without our knowing it. The minute we put wagons behind a loco or run a second train, we have entered railway practice. The reason is simple, we usually do not wish to see train derailments or crashes.

Most railways have their length divided into sections, each guarded by a signal. When a train occupies a section, then no other train can enter it. In the U.K. the length between two such signals is the 'block section'. When the engine driver stops his locomotive at a signal, the train halts along a length of track behind him. This is the 'berth section'. It follows therefore that signals must guard the whole train, and allow an overlap where the front or rear of another train is just entering or clearing a block section.

Shunting and wrong direction movements are common where track or ballast is being laid or maintained. In the U.K. the train normally moves forward on the left

hand track, in the U.S.A. on the right, with the driver's seat across on the right. However, you are master of your own railway!

The newcomer may find it worthwhile to take a closer look at the various forms of remotely controlling the trains and other operations. Simple radio control and multiple train working will need the 'drivers' to be aware of good railway practice, or the sections can have some other built-in form of protection besides signals. *(See the section on electronics)*.

The type of radio-control set commonly used for garden railways is the basic two-function variety used for model boats and cars. The set consists of a transmitter (Tx), two servo actuators, and a receiver (Rx) which will be battery-powered and control the servos. The complete receiver and actuator outfit is small enough to fit into very confined spaces, but we do have box cars and large-bodied diesels where there are cavernous amounts of empty space. REA, Aristo and the larger LGB diesels have a great deal of space for our equipment. We can even include larger sound speakers with the sound generator circuits. The standard, off the shelf radio control units work quite well over the garden distances we normally encounter.

The transmitter will be hand-held, and sends the coded control signals to the receiver's aerial. The receiver is smaller than a match box, as are the surprisingly powerful servos. With the electrical power available to us we do not always need batteries.

Servo motors are a little like car windscreen wipers in that the motor rotates about one turn, and this is translated into a sideways movement of an arm, to open a throttle, actuate a signal or move points. Sometimes a servo can actuate a switch which will in turn cascade to operating several functions at once. This can give a measure of real safety working, where one set of points actuates a second set to prevent collisions or to take a train in and out of a loop, activating signals at the same time.

Control of electrically powered models is different to operating a live-steam locomotive, as we shall see. An electronic speed controller with no moving parts will be used instead. This will plug into the receiver instead of a servo. A 'battery eliminator' will draw operating power from our track source and the controller will regulate the current to the traction motors upon received radio commands. The usual power supply in conjunction with radio control is rechargeable Ni-Cad cells. But with our large current needs, power packs would have to be substantial. This would also take up space in a locomotive or wagon, however this has been done. There are manually set control units deigned for on-board battery traction power. These may have a forward/reverse switch, and a simple push button for 'slow down and stop', mounted in easy reach on the side or roof of the model.

Imagine the environment under the bonnet/hood of your car after an hour's drive – the heat, pumps and other electrical devices switching on and off, hot water and oil. This is the environment that we expect our radio control receivers and associated circuits and devices to work in. This is a radio controlled steam locomotive. The situation is not much better for everyday

electric traction. Poor rail joints, dirty contacts, both causing sparks, and sparks generate radio interference. There is of course a complete absence of not only interference but all radio signals in tunnels. Cuttings or any place that the train is out of sight can cause signal and control loss. So can lumps of metal (lawnmowers) and wet bushes.

By far the greatest number of radio controlled models operate in almost ideal conditions – flying on a clear summer's day, across the smooth surface of a small pond, round a miniature car racing circuit. The models are almost never out of sight and always nearby.

Nothing brings home to us more clearly that we are running a real railway, outside in the real world, it is just smaller. We are fortunate that there are just a few individual manufacturers who build units specifically for us. These will have smoothing circuits so that a spark will not push the throttle wide open, or a 'hold' facility so that the train will keep on doing the same thing when it goes out of sight and radio contact. These days there is much less radio interference for our 'terrestrial' radio uses.

We have two frequency bands at our disposal, the older and more common 27Mhz or the newer and interference free 40Mhz band. 27 Mhz can be used by model arcraft pilots as well as their exclusive 35Mhz band. 27Mhz is prone to all kinds of interference, from model toys, CB radio and there are only six frequencies for everyone.

Converting a small locomotive like IP Engineering's 'Jane' to radio control involves considerable ingenuity. In this case a bunker extension was fitted to house the servo and associated radio equipment beneath a brass plate, on which were glued pieces of coal. The reverser servo crank comes out of the bunker side and is connected to the reverser lever, set by the smokebox, via a bell crank made from silver soldered tube.

40Mhz band is the exclusive province of the surface modeller. Specifications for equipment are high. There is good interference rejection and we have thirty frequencies available to us. When running at home there is no need to worry about frequency conflicts unless you have modelling neighbours. All the component parts come with simple plug together wires.

In truth, all radio control systems can suffer interference, and we railwaymen borrow, where we can, from other modelling clans, such as boats or cars and aeroplanes. Our need is to limit the opportunities for interference with ,among other considerations, good aerial placement. Never leave aerials in a ball. Run them around the inside roof of a wagon, round the top of the tender or the plastic body of a diesel, away from track pick-ups and traction motors. Make sure that you can always see the train or accessory that you are controlling. Always have good batteries.

Although this section is concerned with radio control, it is prudent to suggest that we might try to limit the number of radio controlled operations to, say, moving rolling stock. For instance, there are one or two very good 'station stop' modules that will slow a track powered train and hold it for an adjustable time. This means that the radio controller does not need to do this from a distance.

Another possibility for difficult terrain is the radio control of a main track power controller, housed perhaps in the 'train shed'. Then the 'driver' only needs to keep the aerial mounted there in his line of sight for control, regardless of where the train may be.

We could also limit the functions to two – forward/reverse and fast/slow. Magnets in the track, and reed switches under locomotives, will activate whistle, bell and horn sound units on board. These always sound best when just entering a tunnel.

There are several software packages for computer control of railways. While these are mostly designed for large and complex 'Double-O' or commercial layouts, they are usable for our purposes and also via 'interfaces' that switch on the computer's command. The originator of G Scale, LGB, has an off-the-shelf computer interface to control trains.

In recent years various forms of remote control using modern digital electronics have been marketed. Typically, LGB equipment can be controlled from a hand held (but hard wired) controller for up to eight trains or functions, or eight individually set hand controllers can be plugged into the power supply. Thus the possibility of up to eight trains on the same track, and the same power supply, can be contemplated.

Many model locomotives have a module inside them – a bank of little 'dip-switches' that can be set to accept only signals from one of eight 'channels' on hand controllers. The LGB 'Lenz Multi-Train' system even allows programming from such controllers. The carrier for the individual signals is the current to the track, and the track itself is the conductor of the operating information to each of the units set to a particular channel by the controllers.

Digital and multi-function control means that there can be more than one

Opposite: Radio-controlled live steam locomotives may be expensive but achieve incredible realism. Here are the model and prototype versions of the Welshpool & Llanfair Railway 2-6-2T No. 14, originally built by Hunslet for service in Sierra Leone. The model is by Pearse Locomotives with lining by Lightline.

action triggered by a particular channel. For instance, activating a set of points may also operate a couple of signals, a level crossing gate and a warning bell. In this way, the decision to run a train into a siding may for example also prepare the way and activate all the necessary equipment for tipping wagons. The possibilities clearly are greater in number than the eight basic channels, with perhaps dozens of actions following each other on a single channel!

Another manufacturer, in the USA, has a similar system – 'Train Engineer'. Marklin too, with their newer tinplate railway, have installed digital control, whereby several trains can be controlled by one main (track power) controller. Since the Lionel version many years ago, no one as yet has produced a mock-up of the driver's controls on the footplate or in the diesel cab.

Mobile telephones have had little effect on our operations as yet.

A number of specialists exist, who will convert your motive power to remote or radio operation. It is also possible to buy a box van with all the components fitted ready to plug to the locomotive and control it remotely.

With the advent of the 40Mhz band, and the newer digital controllers, there is a serious challenge to the old 'knob on a box'. So, one can either follow a train around the track, driving it like a real engineman, or, in a spirit of true decadence, relax in a deck chair awaiting the arrival of the 10.45 with a gin and tonic and ice in the box cars.

With garden railways, all things are possible!

6
Live Steam

What is it about a live steam engine that makes such an impact on people? Men, women, and children who express no real interest in trains will stop to watch a steam engine go by. Thousands of people flock to steam centres and to watch special events. Countless books and articles have attempted to analyse the attraction, and one of the essential points seems to be that although a steam engine is only a piece of machinery it appears to have life.

Heat, fire, water, steam, movement, rhythmic noises, and even that unforgettable smell are all the ingredients of a magic concoction that brings a tingle to anyone with a memory of steam in their soul. Part of this memory and love of steam engines is what makes many of us want to recreate our own railway world in miniature.

In the smaller scales most modellers have no option but to represent steam engines in visual outline only, but of necessity the wheels have to be powered by an electric motor hidden inside. However beautiful, these models lack the essential ingredient. They are not self sustaining, generating their own power from fire and water. By moving to the larger scales in the garden we give ourselves the option of running real steam engines. There is a vast range of models available, which operate just like the real thing. There are fewer models that actually burn coal, especially at the lower scales (Gauge I, G Scale) because relatively more expertise is required to drive them; they are really not for the beginner. The use of gas or methylated spirit is our usual introductory fuel.

The garden railway enthusiast must be sure of what he wants from a railway and its locomotives before embarking on what may be an expensive mistake. The prospective purchaser of a steam locomotive should ask the following questions:

● Do I want an instant train service, turned on and off at short notice?
● Do I want to operate a number of trains simultaneously?

The humble British Mamod has introduced many garden railway enthusiasts to live steam. This example has been fitted with a replacement 'Jane' boiler. The cab back has been removed to give a better view of the sight glass and easier access to the meths filler and regulator.

● Am I more interested in complex shunting operations than watching trains running?
● Do I have a line which is very short, or end-to-end, or with sharp curves, steep gradients?

If the answer to most of these is 'yes' then you will be well satisfied with two-rail electric operation, and steam is probably not for you. The other side of the coin, however, needs to be examined:

● Do you like the idea of driving or operating a real steam locomotive?
Are you attracted by the sight, sound, and smell of real steam, as distinct from reproduced sound and synthetic smoke?
● Do you like the idea of preparing a locomotive for a run, and the operations involved in its care?
● Do you also like the idea of getting to know your locomotive ñ and the 'road' – and learning to judge its capabilities under different operating conditions?

A 'yes' to any of these and you are a potential convert to live steam – and an engine driver! With the decision made to buy live steam, you will need to seek advice about your choice. EVERY locomotive is an individual. There are many types, and there are options for manual or radio control. There is no substitute for seeing locomtives in action and using the opportunity to talk things over with enthusiasts. Make contact with a local group, and go along on an open day. Written advice will almost always contain personal preferences but there are a number of points worth bearing in mind.

Most model steam locomotives are virtually hand made, and this does not come cheaply. You can however buy a reliable, powerful locomotive for about the same price as a factory-built top-of-the-range electric model. Because of its low cost, most people began their steam career with the humble British Mamod loco, these are excellent value, but severely limited in performance – in terms of power, slow running ability and duration of run. There are several upgrading conversions with different burner types and radio control.

The first locomotive that you purchase should really be a soundly emgineered product from one of the established manufacturers. Even their basic locomotives will give many years of satisfactory service and pleasure, and probably keep their monetary value as well.

CYLINDERS AND VALVES

The simplest system for converting steam pressure to rotary motion of the wheels is by oscillating cylinders like those on the Mamod. Reversal of these engines is by a rotary valve which also controls the steam quantity to the cylinders, and hence speed. A feature of these cylinders is that they are more efficient at high speeds and so are not so suitable for slow speed (usually narrow gauge) locomotives.

Engines with piston valves can be reversed with a simple adjustment to a rotary valve, whereas engines with slide valves need valve gear to change direction. The simplest form of valve gear is a slip-eccentric and, although this is very reliable, to reverse direction, the locomotive must be pushed a short distance in the intended direction, of travel to set the gear.

Effective reversing gear comes in many shapes and, in principle, a lever in the cab operates rods which set the valves and determine the direction of travel. The various systems, named after their inventors and common in model form, include Hackworth, Stephenson and Joy, with Walschaerts as the most widely used valve gear and giving detailed movement when the loco is in motion.

The performance of locomotives with complex but efficient valve gear such as Walschaerts under radio-control is very close to real life, with satisfactory sounds and steady increases in speed pulling heavy loads away from stations and up gradients.

BOILERS AND BURNERS

Effective steam generation in a steam locomotive is the most important consideration, whatever its size. If it cannot make enough steam, it will not

move or sustain movement with a train. In the prototype, the heat to boil water comes from coal or oil, in models oil is a non-starter and coal boilers are expensive to build and need great skill to operate successfully.

Meths fired engines are usually 'pot-boilers' which have a wick below the boiler – like a kettle. They are simple to operate (by adjusting the wick!) but their performance can suffer in wind and rain unless the flame is well shielded

with a firebox and side tanks.

Gas-fired engines usually burn bottled Butane in a blowlamp type burner, pointing along the centre of a single flue tube surrounded by the boiler's water. Steam can be raised very quickly, and the engine run in all weathers.

Some more expensive engines use more complex ëSmithiesí or fire-tube boilers which have meths or gas flames in a firebox. The fire is drawn through the boiler by the exhaust steam from the cylinders, which is directed up the chimney. Initial steam raising on engines with this type of boiler must be achieved with a small electric fan inserted at the chimney to draw the fire. After about five minutes there should be sufficient steam in the boiler for the engine's own natural steam blower to take over.

Operation of an engine with an internally fired boiler is far more like driving a full sized engine and, although rather complex for a beginner, it can be very rewarding to learn the skills necessary to get the best performance from an engine pulling a heavy train.

Some gas burners can be quite noisy. Refuelling can be difficult, particularly in cold weather which affects the gas pressure. There are also safety aspects which must be respected when storing and handling bottled gases. All live steam operations should involve a healthy respect of burning fuel, boiling

Opposite: The Japanese company, Aster Hobbies, has had a powerful influence on Gauge 1 with its impressive range of steam locomotives. Many are supplied in kit form, as seen in these views of the partly assembled chassis and the completed version of the L&NWR 'Jumbo'.

This page: Waiting for a full head of steam on a coal-fired locomotive built by Philip Holroyd. The sight, sound and smell of coal-firing can be the ultimate garden railway experience but requires skill and patience.

Above: Model or prototype? A second glance is certainly needed at this superb top-of-the-range product from Tolhurst Model Engineering. An exact scale version of the Vale of Rheidol 2-6-2T Owain Glyndwr, it has multi-tube boilers capable of being fired by coal, meths or gas. There is full radio control, not only of the regulator and reverser but also the blower, whistle and draincocks.

Right: Raising pressure – a new 5-inch gauge locomotive undergoes its steam trials.

water, and pressures up to 75 pounds per square inch.

In these few pages it has not been possible to deal with all the aspects of steam locomotive purchase and operations. Whether you opt for a gas fired locomotive with full radio control on the regulator and reverse, or a simple manual slip-eccentric meths fired pot-boiler, as you strike the first match you will open up a whole new world of activity in your garden and beyond.

The cab of Owain Glyndwr has functional controls that are as near to scale as possible. The coal bunker doors slide up and down and the spectacle plates are hinged.

7
Evolution of Your Railway

Every newly constructed railway has a raw, unrealistic look. How long it will take for the railway to mature and blend in with its surroundings depends upon the materials used and how you go about adding character.

A new oval of track laid directly onto a concrete patio floor will always look like an indoor train set. A little extra effort and thought will enable the train set boundaries to be expanded. In the section on track bases we drew attention to the importance of choosing the right materials. These not only determine the initial character of the line but its possibilities. Ballast, for example, immediately places the track visually as part of the permanent scene, and eliminates the impression of rails laid on the ground. A coat of matt brown to the rail sides removes the shiny newness, but they will weather in a short time anyway. Keep the rail top sufaces clean at all times of course.

It is important to keep fresh soil away from the immediate vicinity of the track, otherwise nature soon takes over and trains will be derailed by the jungle growth. Vegetation will only add to the overall effect when it is controlled, and grows where you determine. Keep a barrier between the track ballast and the garden proper to minimise any physical or visual intrusion.

Cement blocks used as a track base (the formation) will weather eventually but can be helped with liquid manure to encourage algae growth – the same applies to fresh rocks. It is also a simple task to put together a weed killer train from tank wagons to spray the track and ballast.

The fine – bladed varieties of hard wearing grass tend to look much better than the broad leaved varieties that also creep. The track base can be extended outwards with alpine chippings in various colours. Together with some spreading alpines, a season's growth should see the railway appear to have been there a much longer time.

Visual disguise of elevated track supports can be made using rocks, grassed embankments, or box and small leaved privet hedging. Walls, fences

Ballast, controlled vegetation and weathered rails all help the railway to blend in with its surroundings. Archangel Princess Hester looks very much at home as it meanders through the tamed wilderness on a corner of the Border Counties Railway.

and garden rubbish can become eyesores against the near perfection of your growing miniature world.

Record photography, a visual diary of the progress, is always a good idea. Photographs from near track height, and at vantages that mimic the real world, will add to the realism. A fast film will allow a small aperture and give increased depth of sharpness to models. A photograph will often direct your attention to a feature that you have become accustomed to, but need to see in a new light.

Bridges are usually so beneficial in setting the scale that it is difficult to have too many. They should appear to have a purpose, and give sufficient clearance for the largest rolling stock. USA 'Old Timers' with wood burning smoke stacks and cabooses all need the full height of your loading gauge. Even a simple wooden pedestrian bridge can be very effective in stirring childhood memories of trains passing beneath. It is quite feasible to make a wooden bridge from square section hardwood, waterproof glue, and panel pins – in a working day, and have trains passing over or under. The materials are in every Do-it-yourself shop.

To avoid disaster, remember that locomotives can weigh over ten pounds,

and some of the big live steamers even more. The wildlife that will use the
railway as a garden corridor can also be quite weighty. Make sure that there
is a strong plank or angle iron imbedded out of sight to form the load-bearing
structure of your bridge. Even small section plastic drainpipes can be solvent
glue welded into bridges that are structurally sound and look real. A suspension

bridge has been made using plastic plumbing pipes and motor cycle chains for the suspension components. Over six feet in span across a stream, the effect is terrific. Concrete bridges, cast 'in-situ' on a hardboard framework, can give elegant arches. Use chicken wire mesh as re-inforcing.

Looking closely at real bridges, you will see that they are all supported on pads or hinges to allow for movement when loads pass over, or temperature. Your bridges should be tailored to the gap that they are spanning and appear to be supported in the same way on abutments at each end. We are still in the real world after all?

Bridge construction is also the basis for turntables.

Both small and large plastic bridges are available from LGB, and there are specialist bespoke manufacturers of aluminium section girder bridges.

Viaducts are a real challenge, especially on curves. These need proper engineering skills and look best at around two feet in height (or more!) The ground on which they are to be built must be consolidated and stable. Good footings (foundations) will be needed, and the ends must abut to the terrain without the possibility of movement. Mistakes are hard to rectify.

Footings for bridge piers in ponds can be tricky but a simple piece of 'know-how' can help. Place a thick sheet of poystyrene foam board on the bottom, a concrete block on this, and there is the foundation for the model. When the pond is constructed along with the railway, a polystyrene sheet under the liner matching the one on top prevents any chance of a water leaking puncture.

Opposite: Record photography is invaluable in keeping a visual diary of progress. The top view shows Martyn Mitchell's G Scale line set in a barren landscape in 1986. Slightly back from the same viewpoint ten years later, the scene is transformed.

This page: It is difficult to have too many bridges as they are so beneficial in setting the scale. Here a home-made through-truss timber bridge is ready for installation.

A further use for bridges is that they can disguise 'lift-out' sections where the line crosses a path or access to a shed. The main problem is electrical continuity. You cannot rely on fishplates here. An electrical feedwire to the section and hidden wire continuing to the next section leaves only the problem of rail alignment. Strength is essential because of wear and tear.

While bridges, embankments and general civil engineering add variety and life to the developing railway, they are potential danger points in case of a derailment. To prevent a valuable locomotive or stock plunging three feet or so to the ground, some form of retention is needed. This can be as simple as a check-rail which is laid next to the running rail but inside the two rails. This keeps the wheels in the track space even if bumping over the sleepers. You will find them in all pointwork for this reason. Our 'master' isolating electrical switch comes in handy for these emergencies.

Parapet walls at various heights made of weather proof materials – ABS plastic, fibreglass or resin, concrete or plastic foam – can be modelled or purchased. Low fences can be made from wire strung between little wooden posts or upright sleepers. Be careful that a fence itself cannot damage the stock. Fences are quite difficult to model, and can look like a prison perimeter. Pola and others make various types for farm and zoo models that suit our purpose as well.

Cuttings into 'hillsides' serve as an excuse for an overbridge over the line. Provide drainage because they can also flood. Visually they can be disappointing, but where there is scope for rapid changes in levels, there is no doubt that the sight of a train leaving a tunnel then running through a cutting out onto an embankment is difficult to equal for realism. Cuttings also provide protection from the wind ñ trains can derail in strong gusts in exposed line sections. Heed the warning of a wind-gauge sited on the Owencarrow viaduct after the 1905 disaster!

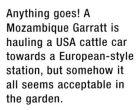

Anything goes! A Mozambique Garratt is hauling a USA cattle car towards a European-style station, but somehow it all seems acceptable in the garden.

8
Giving your Railway its own Character

Does your developing railway look like all the others you have seen? Is the stock, like others, straight from the catalogue? If you are a true collector, or reproducing a particular line from manufactured items, and your intention is to collect one example of each item boxed and mint, then this section is not for you.

However, if you want to create your own distinctive railway, with its own unique identity, you can achieve this with a little thought and effort. There is the dilemma that you will have just paid a great deal of money for an engine or rake of coaches, and do not want to risk spoiling them or lowering their value. The answer is to start with small items that are inexpensive, secondhand, or well used already. We have previously mentioned Playmobil and Lehmann (LGB) 'Toy Train' – the inexpensive versions of the LGB marque. These are a favourite for repainting with enamel model paints, modifying with ABS glue. The model railway and war game diorama magazines often feature weathered models and 'how to do it' features – as, of course, does the specialist garden railway press.

The Bachmann inexpensive items can easily be 'improved' with a silver paint pen applied to black plastic wheel rims. The simplest models to disassemble are the inexpensive ones. If you are more experienced and careful, LGB itself will reward an imaginative conversion with custom waterslide transfers for lettering and logos. Many locomotives, even mighty Beyer-Garratts, have been fashioned from LGB components ñ and a piece of drainpipe for a boiler!

Two modern adhesive materials have joined the ubiquitous polystyrene

cement for modelling: adhesive and gap filling foam – in spray cans, and automotive body filler – which will join metals and non-greasy plastics. This two-part resin with filler works under water too. A similar two-part material, milliput, will join metal to plastic.

If you have a narrow gauge line in the making and you are building a miniature version of a favourite prototype, whether a slate quarry, sugar cane plantation, Swiss mountains, or Atlantic islands – there are specialist books and societies for your guidance, and many off-the-shelf models.

Most manufacturers produce beautiful models which are often close-to-scale replicas of real locomotives, coaches or wagons. LGB, for instance, models fifty different railways, much of which did not run together and was of different gauges. The important thing here is that you make the rules for your railway, and you are free to do as you wish.

Manufacturers have a tendency to paint things with a bright glossy finish or leave bright self-coloured plastic which is intended to appeal to the potential buyer. One look at most working railways, even preserved ones, shows that very soon the coaches and wagons acquire a patina of work use, especially around track level.

Take care that paints are compatible with the plastic and avoid cellulose based automotive spray cans – they will either dissolve existing paint finishes, form a 'crazed' surface or not stick at all. The secret of good painting is the preparation by masking off the areas not to receive paint. Masking tapes and

Effective weathering needs courage but is a key factor in giving a line character and a 'real-life' look.

Opposite: Locomotives as they really were! This coal-fired 0-4-0ST from Shawe Steam Services creates wonderful clag.

This page: A suitably weathered Porter and Climax on the Montezuma Lumber Company's logging line. All the work has been hand-done by Brian Coldicott of Locofinish and has stood up well to the wear and tear of live steam.

Train of scratchbuilt
Ffestiniog Railway rolling
stock.

newspaper takes a long time to arrange as a mask, and a quick pass with the paint spray lasts a few seconds. The trouble is worth it for the finish. Use light coats, let them dry and build up the colour. When you are attempting to weather stock to make it appear more realistic, conduct some research first in the magazines.

One interesting fact is that motor cars, and trains, use several types of black – not just matt, satin, egg shell and gloss. Be careful when painting coal. There are several replica paints for metal surfaces, from brushed aluminium to brass and gun metal – for massive locomotive castings such as pony trucks.

One feature that really creates a railwayís identity and character is having your own railway name. One or two well known modellers have christened their lines with names such as 'Lake George & Boulder' to fit the LGB initials. In most cases it will mean removing the original painted or transferred letters with a scraper blade or fine 'wet & dry' abrasive. Careful matching of colours may allow painting over the lettering and a whole area. There are also replica matching colours for most of the major railways.

Nameplates in brass with locomotive names or your railway motif are quite cheap and easy to obtain through specialist dealers. Another valuable aid for those with waterslide transfers is a softener which makes the transfer fit snugly over rivets and planking. Decal-set is a product which will do this. Always cover applied lettering with the protective coating to prevent wear effects (Decal-cote).

Avoid high gloss unless you dismantle and prepare in great detail the surfaces to be treated. Study motor car repair manuals for painting tips. Weathering will not disguise a poor paint job. Avoid lining engines and coaches yourself. Even press on lines are difficult to attach properly to detailed scale models.

All of this must have drawn you to the conclusion that the ultimate way to create your own railway company is totally to repaint the stock in your own

Top: Massive centre cab Co-Co diesel built by Trevor Shephard for his garden line, sited just a couple of miles from Swinden Quarry, near Skipton, where the prototype is regularly in use. Weighing no less than 150 tons, it is reputedly the most powerful locomotive in Europe in relation to its size.

Lower: Intriguing Fairlie-style locomotive on a New Zealand line, fashioned from a pair of LGB 'Stainz' 0-4-0s.

Corporate identity as epitomised on the Chemin de Fer Ardennais, a modern-image line inspired by French and Swiss metre-gauge practice. The locomotive and coaches are all scratchbuilt from plastic. Note the snowplough on No. 75 – a first defence against debris on the line.

colours with a distinct house livery for coaches, wagons and locomotives. The American railroads, perhaps more than the European ones, used to paint their crack express trains in distinctive liveries. You could run just one train in your own special chosen livery and keep your day to day operations for common stock straight from the catalogue. The 'Daylights' – West Coast USA expresses in various colours, mostly black, orange, brown and red – the Blue Train of South Africa, and the silver coloured 'Silver Jubilee' are all examples. The Eurostar trains running from London to Paris and Brussels under the English Channel, and Virgin trains distinctive red and black livery, can easily be applied to the latest high speed train models from Lehmann, who also make a 'Blue Train' and Pullman carriages for the Orient Express.

With professional lettering and light weathering to your crack express the railway will truly come alive.

You are probably itching to grab a hacksaw and start 'kit-bashing'. You can remove or super – detail, to emphasise your corporate image, as you wish. Again, start with simple change and follow photographs for detailed highlights, cab roofs, ventilators or steps. 'Plasticard' sheets at around .020in are useful in white, black or clear, with surface detail such as planks, roof tiles or smooth. Experience with this material, and plastic sections such as girders, rods or tubes, will lead you on to bigger things such as buildings and even to scratchbuilding rolling stock or locomotives.

9
Buildings and Accessories

There seem to be two schools of thought regarding the incorporation of buildings into the garden scenery. There are those who would add one or two important structures, such as a a station or signal box, and those who accumulate whole villages populated with very active little people engaged in all sorts of industry, as well as working on the railway. Luckily, there are products to suit the most dedicated real estate developer and industrial entrepreneur.

BUILDINGS AND PEOPLE

Some of the most useful garden railway buildings come from Pola, which are those used in the LGB catalogue illustrations. Pola buildings often come as self-coloured, simple glue together kits. They are made of weather-resistant plastic and are quite convincing from a distance. As well as the Swiss and American old time station buildings, there are farm and circus productions, and 'specials' such as limited edition working sawmills. The water towers that

'Clear Water' depot and a Durango & Silverton water tower – two buildings in the extensive range of US-style kits by Piko.

Time for a chat! The figures
outside the 'stone' locomotive
shed were made from
Fimo, a plastic modelling
material obtainable from
good art shops in a wide
range of colours.

The station scene, portrayed by a new and expanding range of British outline buildings.

work, to replenish locomotives, or their drivers with something a little stronger, are very popular. A similar range of kits is also made by Piko.

A drawback is that the mass market for these products is continental Europe and the USA. It has been left to a small number of U.K. based manufacturers to produce a few British outline buildings in coursed stone. A new range of British outline buildings in brick, brick and stone, flint and brick, and random stone is on the market and the range is expanding. This should stimulate interest in the cradle of railways – Great Britain up to the post war era at the time of mixed steam and diesel working.

Almost all railways begin and end in major urban areas, with town or village buildings whose existence is due to the railway. Major works such as Doncaster, Swindon and Crewe created their own townships. Transporting freight encouraged industry at railheads. Trams carried the people around the towns.

All railways need stations, signal boxes, engine and goods sheds. For us, they are good hiding places for section or points switches and loudspeakers relaying trains sounds and announcements.

The realism that we crave for on our small railways can be destroyed when we run an expensive live steam LNER *Mallard* with a rake of teak-sided coaches into a station with a Swiss outline, or set a 1950s' Aristo FA1 diesel and aluminium-sided observation coaches against a Wild West village.

All of these buildings will benefit from the addition of lighting, and some can have chimneys adapted to smoke using the same mechanism as the locomotives, but with continuous whisps rather than the expected puffs – where

Many outdoor modellers have created whole villages, turning the railway into almost a secondary feature. Pontfaen has been described as 'an evocation to small scale of the impact of the railway age upon communities'. The buildings are of simple construction, using softwood and oil paint, with plastic sheet and corrugated tin -- salvaged from meat tins! – as roofing.

the hot oil is heated into smoke by a hot wire using 18 volts AC or track voltage.

Although toy-like, Playmobil (which uses LGB track) has kit buildings and little people – including railway workers – engaged in a host of activities. Adventure toys include working speedboats, canoes, dockside cranes and big fire engines – some quite realistic and all in G Scale, a wonderful way of introducing children to our small fresh-air world. There is even a radio-controlled toy train. This means that children can invite friends to share their railway and take it over without fear of damage. The railway itself can be a learning environment and encourage team activities. In any event, who will carry the baton when the older of us retire from the scene?

The most impressively modelled Gauge 1 and G Scale/G64 (Gauge 3) figures come from Preiser, much used in architectural modelling, but the list from all railway manufacturers is growing.

Station platforms, not always used on the continent of Europe or the USA, but mandatory in the UK, can be formed from concrete poured into a makeshift mould about 25mm high for G Scale then painted with roofing bitumen for tarmac. The widest wagon must have clearance, and beware of curves, however slight. Platforms will very likely be about fifteen feet long for a terminus, as yet unavailable (LGB has produced a modern Inter-City high-speed

Above: Convincing rural station on the Tincroft Valley Railway in Cornwall. The figures, luggage, lamp and post box all contribute to the effectiveness of the scene.

Lower: Garden railways take on their own very special magic by night, particularly if attention is given to proper lighting. Carriage shed lights on the Tamarside Railway reflect from the running rails and illuminate the serried ranks of rolling stock. A passing train has its brake van and rear lamp lit by battery power.

multiple unit encouraging us to be up-to-date) and so we tend to model halts and country stations – another pressure away from the main line and towards narrow gauge?

MISCELLANEOUS ACCESSORIES

What else could we call this section? – we needed a 'catch-all' for some of the things that did not fit neatly elsewhere. We also needed to draw your attention to the really enormous range of garden railway bits and pieces that in all probability rivals the smaller gauges, and when true costs are measured may not cost a great deal more for the massive increase in model size and detail. Our hobby, which is truly international, is as well served as the traditional indoor scales. A browse through the back numbers of garden railway magazines and catalogues will reveal all.

To whet your appetite, and assist with the decision of which way to go with your own railway's style, a look around the shelves of a major garden railway specialist produced the following choice items that caught our eye at random:

- A working tipping bogie wagon system.
- Three different level crossings, one with lights and bells, and train activated barriers.
- Bags of wagon loads – barrels, boxes, oil drums.
- An electronic auto-shuttle to make a train or tram go back and forth, a simple unit in a buffer stop, another with auto slow down under full control.
- Electronic digital diesel and steam sound units to fit into locomotives and wagons.
- Signals, British and Continental, moving arm or lights, all working.
- Station accessories in white metal – buckets, sweet machines, benches.
- More than two British signal boxes – in brick or stone.
- Viaduct arch modules in concrete or plastic.
- Bags of unpainted figures, sitting or standing.
- A large number of publications and books relating to the hobby.
- Garden railway videos.

10
Plants for the Railway

To many people the garden may be as important as the railway that they are creating within it. The reason that garden matters do not occupy half of this book is simply because of the wealth of botanical and horticultural information and also the readily available expertise in books and magazines.

Having a railway in the garden gives the avid gardener even more niches and different planting habitats with which to experiment, which is as good a reason as any for starting a garden railway project. When considering plants for the miniature railway scenery, it is obviously important to think small, not only in height and spread of plant but also in leaf size.

Probably the most important task when 'greening' the railway is to give some structure, using miniature trees. There are numerous dwarf conifers and evergreens which provide all-the-year colour and interest. It is vital when selecting your trees to check carefully that they are truly dwarf, and not just slow growing varieties. When chosing, consider the size of the leaves for proportion, spreading habit (if any), rate of growth (in your soil) and overall shape. Some specimens can be made more tree like (hence less shrub like) by removing the lower branches and revealing the 'trunk'.

Shrubs such as Box (Buxus) and Lonicera Nitida can be planted and trimmed to create miniature trees or even hedges. Cuttings of these are easy to take and grow quickly into more of the same. Use any clippings as your cuttings.

There are also some miniature flowering shrubs which can enhance a railway. Some of the Hebes are excellent, with small leaves, flowers and compact growth habit. They vary in colour and shape of foliage, so choose carefully. Some Potentillas can be kept trim and provide colour, with small dog-rose shaped blooms all summer. They have tiny narrow leaves, but with the disadvantage of being leafless all Winter. For those fortunate enough to have an acid soil, dwarf Azaleas can look like stunning full sized Rhododendrons to the passengers on your railway. Miniature roses,

'Greening' the railway.

Opposite, top: Careful planting either side of the line gives the illusion that this Roundhouse 'Millie' is emerging from mixed woodland on the Ambledown Valley Railway. *Lower:* A miniature tree separates pond from main line on the Gauge 1 Combe Down line. Its owner refers to this stretch as 'my Teignmouth sea wall'.

This page: Scenes on the Longlands & Western Railway, noted for its perfect narrow gauge atmosphere, with ground-cover plants creeping across the tracks and trains appearing to run among the trees.

especially the ground cover varieties, can also be effective. Euonymus evergreens, if kept in trim, can provide welcome variegated evergreen foliage to act as a foil to often shorter-lived flowering plants. Euonymus is also useful around off-the-ground lines.

Heathers are versatile plants and can be found in a wide selection of foliage colour from yellow to deep blue-green, which may also vary through the seasons. However, these must be selected carefully as many cannot tolerate limey soils. If in doubt about your soil or if you have imported soil from your engineering works, use a pH tester kit from a garden centre. With limey alkaline soil, your choice of Heathers will be limited to the winter-flowering Ericas. If your soil is acid, then plan Erica and Calluna varieties. Once you have planted these in light, peaty soil, give them a good 'haircut' after flowering to keep their compact shape. Heathers can spread quickly and can look straggly if not kept in trim.

Many alpines and plants recommended for rockeries will fit into the railway scene, especially if they are used for growing in cracks and crevices of walls and rockery scenery. It is impossible to name here all those species which are suitable, but some favourites – easily available – are described.

Try a yellow spring flowering, grey-leaved Alyssum Montanum growing down an embankment. This is smaller and neater than the more familiar Allysum Saxitale. Contrast this with varieties of white or purple Arabis or Aubretia which can also be found with variegated leaves. Even when not in flower, these plants provide an attractive mound of foliage all year. Some low-growing varieties of campanula also provide this foliage interest and have small bell-like flowers in summer. They have the added advantage of seeding and spreading themselves into the smallest cracks and crevices of paving and walls.

For sunny banks you cannot beat the Helianthemums which have a splendid spreading show of colour, their blooms being similar to Potenetilla but with the advantage of being evergreen. They also grow easily from cuttings. Other plants suitable for growing down sunny banks or for creating a spreading mound are Dianthus, phlox (alpine variety), saxifrages, Sedums and Sempervivums.

The Sedums are also suitable for small areas near the track and stations which might be looking bare. This varied genus is very good tempered; pieces can be uprooted and put down even where there is little soil, and then soon take root and spread. Some may be invasive, but can easily be controlled.

The Sempervivums are equally useful. It is best to select these carefully, rejecting the large dramatic rosetted varieties which could be more daunting than a triffid to a small station master! These too can be uprooted. Remove a rosette, make a small hole or poke the root into a crevice, and the plant will soon begin to spread, making an attractive mound of rosettes.

Herbs can also find a place near the railway, and be useful for the kitchen too. Many of them have small leaves, and penetrating scents. Thymes have

small leaves and can vary from gold/green and silver to dark green, with tiny purple or white blossoms. When crushed or walked upon, the leaves release a delightful perfume, as does Camomile, used in the past for whole lawns, and could be ideal for that railway cutting where grass trimming is a chore.

Several shrubs can be trimmed to create miniature hedges, as here on Peco's 16mm scale line at Beer in Devon. 'Millie' is hauling a rake of Brandbright coaches.

In the autumn, bulbs can be planted, but again, check carefully that the plants will be the right proportion to the railway. Graduate the plant sizes outward from the smallest at the trackside to miniature Daffodils, Narcissi, Rockery Tulips, Crocus, Scillas and Anemone Blanda. Then in spring you will have a blaze of colour for the first train out of the shed.

Last, but not least, do not forget the annual, which can provide instant colour and cover for the new railway, and patch any gaps. Faithfuls such as Alyssum and blue Lobelia – including the trailing varieties with yellow Tagetes- can be very effective, forming clumps of colour throughout the summer. Annuals with larger blooms that grow with taller stems look out of place and proportion to a miniature railway. If you are lucky, some annuals will self-seed, and save you the job the following year.

There are several ways to incorporate garden and railway, including the obvious rockery, the scree-bed based upon peat and gravel, a peat wall or raised bed, a water garden with streams and a track along a dry stone wall around the garden edge. Running the railway around corners usually sterilises a piece of ground behind the track into the corner. This is a niche ideal for

a small rockery, together with a small tunnel if you are ambitious.

Apart from planting out annuals at the end of May, alpines, shrubs, trees and perennials are best planted in the autumn or early spring so that they can become established before the drier summer weather. Autumn is a good time to undertake railway engineering and landscaping together. You will know where the existing planting is, and the ground will have consolidated so that works will not be built upon shifting foundations.

If you can manage to position buildings and plant appropriate foliage around or near them, they will take on a permanence. The whole railway, planting and all, will blossom forth the following spring – even if steam traction is a little later in coming to the line.

Opposite, top: Rockeries are a favourite way of blending together the railway and the garden. In this example the tunnel mouth and trestle bridge are from Garden Railway Specialists. Locomotives are all LGB, as is the girder bridge being crossed by the White Pass & Yukon diesel.

Opposite, lower: Summer glory. A Roundhouse 'Argyll', lined out by Lightline, is coupled to a Leek & Manifold coach with characteristic ornate balcony.

This page: Planting in progress, with Valerie Pratt placing a miniature rose next to the tunnel. Saxifrage and Corsican mint surround the signal.

Conclusion

Trains through the window – with all sorts of action taking place outdoors.

This book has been distilled from the knowledge of the most experienced outdoor model railway builders and contributors to *GardenRail* magazine. We hope that you can employ and adapt their advice and ideas to your own efforts in building and running your own garden railway. Whether a simple circuit or the beginning of a larger scheme, we all started somewhere.

All gardeners share a great gift - patience. Predetermined seasons follow one another in (roughly) the same order, acorns become oaks. So it is with a garden railway. There is much planning, some earthworks and construction, mistakes can be rectified or incorporated into very personal and individual endeavour. For a great many of us, a train journey, or waiting for a local train and watching an express thunder past on a main line, will be the point that we can refer back to, the dream that we are trying to re-create for ourselves.

We hope that in this book there has been something for everyone, horticulturalist or engineer, and for the individual or family, the ideas will be buzzing in your heads, the dream will be taking shape. Although this is an outdoor pursuit, in all weathers – indoors we can undertake construction, electronics, customising and building, and that universal enjoyment – planning for the future.

Glossary

Ballast. Holds track in position, usually granite white chippings not rounded stones. The ballast locks the sleepers in position to keep the track in place, and elevated at the outside of fast curves. Heaped up at sleeper ends to form the 'shoulders'. Allows drainage. Sits on top of the levelled formation.

Battery Eliminator. Circuit to provide a smaller voltage, from low voltage, in place of Ni-Cad rechargeable batteries usually.

Blades. Moving pointed ends of rails in turnouts.

Block. A length of track which can be isolated from the next. In the prototype this is controlled by signals, allowing only one train to occupy the block.

Blower. A suction fan for creating the updraught through a steam engine boiler from the firebox.

Bogies. Swivelling frame holding the running wheels/axles of rolling stock. In the USA 'Trucks'.

Buffers. Found across the ends of the frame in rolling stock. Fixed to a 'Buffer Beam'. The buffers take the shock of shunting or pushing. Usually sprung for shock absorbtion. Can be centrally mounted - one buffer, or one at each side of the beam.

IP Engineering's 'Jane', adapted to take radio control.

Buffer Stop. A heavy weight to absorb impact at the end of tracks to prevent trains running off.

Bullhead. Figure-of-eight section rail.

Caboose (USA). Guard's Van.

Catenary. The downward curve a wire makes when held at the ends. The suspension cable between masts that supports the suspended contact wire for overhead electricity collection.

Chair. Fixed to a sleeper at each end, holds the rail in place.

Couplings. Various devices by which a train is hooked together. In the UK a hook on each buffer beam and a loop or link of steel. In the US and others 'Buck-eye' couplings (as two hands in a pulling grip) also act as buffers. These 'stiffen' the train in the event of a crash.

Diamond. Two tracks crossing at an angle.

Fine-Scale. Very accurate modelling to scale.

Fishplate. Joiner at the ends of rail. From the early 'fish bellied' rails - thicker webs in the centre of a length.

Flange. Raised rim of the wheel which keeps the tread of the wheel on the rail.

Flat-bottomed rail. Upside down T-shaped rail.

Footings. Foundations for construction.

Frog. V-section at the split of rails in turnouts.

Gauge. The distance between the running rails.

Gondola (USA). Low-sided bogie freight wagon.

Hypatufa. Cement, sand and peat. Simulates soft old rock.

Meths (Methylated Ethanol). Methylated Spirit or industrial alcohol.

Pilot (USA). A 'cowcatcher'. (UK) A second locomotive assisting another.

Pot-Boiler. A simple steam generator where the water in the container (boiler) is heated by a flame underneath - like a kettle.

Prototype. The real railways and paraphernalia that we model.

Rack. Toothed rail between the running rails of a rack railway.

Rail Bonding. To provide an electrical path to the adjoining rail.

Rolling Stock. Wagons, carriages, sometimes locomotives.

Section. A Block.

Shoulder. Heaped ballast at ends of sleepers to stop sideways movement.

Signal Box (USA - Switch Tower). Where the signalman controls points and signals.

Sleepers (USA Cross-Ties). Rail support and for maintaining the correct gauge.

Spike (USA). Rails are 'spiked' directly onto sleepers. (UK). Holds chair to sleeper.

Switch (USA). Points, turnouts.

Switch Stand (USA). Point lever.

Switcher (USA). Shunting engine.

Terracotta. Italian for 'burnt earth'. Unglazed fired pottery in a distinctive red colour.

Transformer. Voltage changing device. Two strands of wire, unconnected, wound around a metal core.

Trolley Wire. Simple overhead electricity supply system. Often for trams and trolley buses.

Turnout. Points.

Valve Gear. Mechanism of rods for operating steam valves on an engine, to change direction.

DAVID PRATT

A contributor to *GardenRail* magazine since its first issue, David's engineering skills were honed in the Chief Engineer's Department at Paddington in the last days of steam. His garden railways have always been noted for their authenticity, with track using transitional curves in order to give that elusive 'looks right' touch. Recently he has set up Garden Railway Services, designing and building outdoor lines for those who lack the time or some of the skills, and also providing a maintenance and upgrading service. David is also a qualified industrial photographer.

DAVID JOY

Founded *GardenRail* magazine in 1993 along with Trevor Ridley, the designer of this book, remaining its editor and publisher for the next eight years. Bravely and stubbornly operates a G Scale line 750ft up in the wild and windswept Pennines. A passionate enthusiast of narrow gauge railways in such far-flung locations as Darjeeling and Durango, Patagonia and Portmadoc, he now edits Atlantic's sister magazine *Narrow Gauge World*.

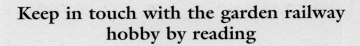